LETTERS TO WORKING PROFESSIONALS

LESSONS ON LIFE, CAREER AND EVERYTHING IN BETWEEN

DR. ASHISH GUPTA

To every working professional
who has a dream to do something bigger than their job
title,
something that lights them up,
something that leaves a mark—
This book is for you.

To those who are quietly building,
who show up even when it's hard,
who tries again after every setback,
and who carry both ambition and anxiety in their
backpacks—
You are seen, and you are not alone.

May these letters remind you of your strength,
reignite your purpose,
and help you turn your daily hustle into a meaningful
journey.

With all my heart,
Ashish

Contents

Contents

Preface

We spend nearly one-third of our lives at work—chasing goals, meeting deadlines, navigating office politics, attending meetings, switching roles, and wondering if we're really moving forward or just moving in circles.

In my years of working with students, young professionals, and seasoned leaders, I've come to realize this:
No one really prepares you for the real world of work.
We're taught how to pass exams, how to write resumes, and how to answer interviews.
But rarely are we taught how to manage pressure, how to deal with setbacks, how to find meaning in our careers, or how to simply survive Mondays.

This book is an attempt to fill that gap—one letter at a time.

It's a natural extension of two of my previous books: Letters to Teenagers and Letters to College Students.
That journey began with helping young minds navigate self-doubt, choices, and identity.
Now, it continues with you—the working professional who's figuring out life while trying to build a career.

This book isn't a manual. It's not a list of hacks.
It's a collection of real, honest letters—filled with the lessons I wish someone had told me earlier. Lessons are drawn from experience, mistakes, conversations, observations, and deep reflection.

Some letters will speak to your ambition.

Some to your exhaustion.
Some to your values.
Some to your vision.

And I hope at least a few will speak to your heart.

You can read this book in sequence or flip to any letter that resonates with where you are right now. There's no right way to read it—only your way.

If this book makes you pause and reflect, if it helps you realign with your purpose, or even if it simply makes you feel less alone in your professional journey, then it has served its purpose.

You're not just a professional with a job.
You're a human being with a story.
And that story deserves to be lived with intention, joy, and courage.

Let's begin.

With sincerity and strength,
Dr. Ashish Gupta

A Letter From The Author

Dear Working Professional,

You're reading this because you're navigating the real world—the one that starts after college, comes without a guidebook, and often demands answers to questions you never thought to ask.

This book is a continuation of a journey that began with Letters to Teenagers, where I spoke to young hearts dreaming about the future. It continued with Letters to College Students, guiding them through the crucial transition of self-discovery and choices. Now, I'm writing to you—the one who stepped out into the world, resume in hand, dreams in eyes, and reality hitting hard.

This book is my honest, experience-soaked letter to you—not as an expert, but as a fellow traveler who has faced his fair share of missed promotions, difficult bosses, self-doubt, sleepless nights, Monday blues, and career reinventions. I've learned that building a career isn't just about climbing the ladder. It's about building character along the way. It's not just about chasing goals, but also about finding meaning, managing emotions, and creating a life that feels fulfilling, not just "successful" in society's eyes.

If you're feeling stuck, confused, burnt out, underappreciated, or even just curious about what comes next—this book is for you.

These letters are not lectures. They are reflections—short, sharp, and sincere. They will challenge you, comfort you, and sometimes just sit with you like a good friend. Read them in order, or jump to the one that calls out to you. Carry it to work, read it during a break, revisit it during a life transition.

Remember, your career is a part of your life. Not your whole life.
And your job is not your identity—it's just one of the ways you express it.

You are not alone in this journey.
Let's walk together.

With honesty and hope,
Ashish

Why I Wrote To You

Because I've been where you are.

I know what it feels like to question your choices at 28.
To chase deadlines that never end.
To wonder if switching jobs is progress or just escape.
To feel excited on Friday and anxious on Sunday night.
To look successful on LinkedIn but feel lost inside.

This phase of life—what we call the "working professional" stage—is perhaps the most underrated yet overwhelming part of our journey. You're expected to have it all figured out. Career, finances, relationships, mental health, physical fitness, social life—and all with a smile.

But the truth is, most of us are learning while living. Making it up as we go. Failing silently. Carrying invisible weights. And waiting for a sign, a voice, or a simple nudge that says, "It's okay. You're doing fine. And you're not alone."

That's why I'm writing to you.

Not to give you a formula. But to share what I've seen, felt, messed up, and learned along the way. These letters are written to remind you that you're not behind. That growth is messy. And that it's okay to pause, reflect, and choose a different path—even in your 30s or 40s.

I wrote this book for the young manager overwhelmed by leadership,
the creative stuck in a job that doesn't feel right,

**the high-performer who still doubts their worth,
and the quiet struggler who's trying to hold it all
together.**

If even one letter makes you feel seen, heard, or hopeful
again, this book has done its job.

Keep going.
I'm rooting for you.

Warmly,
Ashish

How To Read This Book

This book is not a cover-to-cover manual. It's a collection of letters—each one a conversation, a moment of reflection, a pause in your busy life.

You don't have to read it in order.
You don't need a highlighter or a notebook.
You just need a quiet moment and an open heart.

Each letter touches a different aspect of your life as a working professional—career confusion, toxic workplaces, personal growth, relationships, money, burnout, success, and meaning. You can read one letter a day. Or read five in one sitting. Come back to them when life feels heavy, or when you're at a crossroads.

Think of this book as a mirror, a mentor, and sometimes, a friend.
Let the letters speak to you. Let them sit with you.

There's no right way to read this book—
Only your way.

And if any letter truly resonates with you, pass it on.
Because chances are, someone in your circle needs to read it too.

Welcome to the journey.

Ashish

About The Author

Dr. Ashish Gupta is a career coach, educator, author, and changemaker committed to helping people unlock their full potential—personally and professionally.

With over 14 years of experience in higher education and career development, Ashish has guided thousands of students and working professionals through some of life's most important transitions. He has worked with India's top universities, built future-ready programs, and trained teams in admissions, outreach, and communication.

He is also the author of the widely loved books Letters to Teenagers and Letters to College Students—this third installment, Letter to Working Professionals, continues that mission by speaking directly to those navigating the hustle, hopes, and hard truths of modern work life.

Ashish writes the way he coaches—with honesty, empathy, and practical insight.
When he's not mentoring or writing, you'll find him having chai-fueled conversations about purpose, leadership, and the rise of a new India.

You can connect with Ashish at:
www.ashishgupta.co.in
authorashishgupta@gmail.com
LinkedIn: https://www.linkedin.com/in/theashishgupta/

PART I: Finding Your Foundation

CHAPTER I

Welcome to the Real World

Dear Friend,

So, here you are.

Out of the classroom, into the conference room.
Out of theory, into targets.
Out of grades and GPAs, into goals and KPIs.

Welcome to the real world.

This world doesn't come with a syllabus. No set curriculum. No one tells you exactly what's expected of you, and no one hands you a report card every semester. Here, success is undefined. Growth is unstructured. And learning? It never ends.

In college, you could skip a lecture.
Here, you skip a deadline—you pay the price.
In college, you had friends around all the time.
Here, your calendar decides your conversations.
In college, failure was a lesson.
Here, it feels like a label.

It's overwhelming. It's exciting. It's exhausting. And it's real.

But let me tell you this—**you're not supposed to have it all figured out right now.** The world might expect you to.

LinkedIn might pretend to. But growth isn't linear, and life isn't a race.

The real world will challenge you—not just with work, but with self-doubt, comparison, and confusion. You'll question your path. You'll wonder if you're in the right job, the right city, the right life. And that's normal. That's part of the journey.

Here's what I want you to remember:

- **It's okay to feel lost.** You're not alone.
- **It's okay to change directions.** Careers are not train tracks—they're rivers.
- **It's okay to slow down.** Rest is not failure.

Just keep showing up.
Keep learning.
Keep becoming.

You'll figure it out—one decision, one mistake, one breakthrough at a time.

Welcome to the real world.
It's not easy.
But it's where you grow into the person you're meant to be.

And trust me—you're going to be amazing.

Cheering for you,
Ashish

CHAPTER II

Don't Just Work, Build a Career

Dear Friend,

Clocking in. Clocking out. Completing tasks. Attending meetings. Chasing deadlines.
At first, that's what work looks like. You show up, do what's asked, and go home.

But soon, the days blur.
Weeks pass by.
And you begin to wonder—**"Am I just working, or am I building something?"**

Let me tell you something hard but true:
If you don't build your career intentionally, someone else will build it for you—and you may not like where it leads.

There's a big difference between working a job and shaping a career. A job pays the bills. A career builds your future. A job gives you tasks. A career gives you direction. A job may feel safe. But a career pushes you to grow.

So how do you build a career, not just work?

- **Start by asking 'why'** – Why this job? Why this industry? Why this path? Clarity is your compass.
- **Choose learning over comfort** – Don't just stick to what you know. Go where you grow.

- **Say yes to things outside your role** – That's where real growth lies.
- **Find mentors, not just managers** – People who invest in your development, not just your output.
- **Reflect often** – What are you good at? What drains you? What excites you?

A career is not built in a year. It's built in moments—when you speak up in a meeting, when you take ownership of a project, when you choose courage over convenience, when you go the extra mile even when no one is watching.

You can do average work and stay invisible for years.
Or you can start thinking like a professional who's not just passing time, but **creating a life of meaning, impact, and growth.**

So don't just survive your job.
Design your career.

Your future self will thank you.

With purpose,
Ashish

CHAPTER III

Set Goals, Not Just Targets

Dear Friend,

Every quarter, your manager may hand you **targets**—numbers to hit, deadlines to meet, tasks to check off.

But I want to ask you something deeper:
What are your goals?

Not the company's.
Not your boss's.
Yours.

Targets are external—they belong to your job.
Goals are internal—they belong to your life.

Targets focus on what must be done this month.
Goals focus on who you want to become this decade.

Don't get me wrong—targets are important. They keep businesses running. But if you only live by targets, you'll spend years being productive without ever feeling purposeful.

That's how people end up successful... and still feel stuck.

So how do you move beyond just meeting targets and start setting meaningful goals?

- **Define what success means to you**—not your parents, not society, not your peers. You.
- **Set goals that excite and scare you**—because growth lives outside your comfort zone.
- **Balance career goals with life goals**—title and salary matter, but so do health, relationships, and happiness.
- **Break big goals into small habits**—dreams become reality only when broken down into consistent action.
- **Write them down**—not for a vision board, but for your personal blueprint.

You're not just an employee. You're an architect of your future.

Every year, every role, every project—should be a step toward something that matters to you.

Remember, the most fulfilled professionals aren't the ones who hit the most targets.

They're the ones who knew why they were working in the first place.

So, today, take 15 minutes.

Close your laptop.

Open a journal.

And write down your goals—not just what you want to do, but who you want to be.

Your targets will help you succeed at work.

But your goals?

They'll help you succeed in life.

With clarity, Ashish

CHAPTER IV

Know Yourself Before Knowing the Industry

Dear Friend,

The first thing we're told when we enter the workforce is:
"Understand the industry."
Study the trends, learn the tools, know the big players.

That's good advice. But here's better advice—**know yourself first.**

Because if you don't know who you are,
even the best industry won't bring you fulfillment.
Even the highest salary won't feel enough.
Even a great opportunity will feel like a burden.

Too many people become experts in their sector
but remain strangers to themselves.

They know the market.
They don't know their motives.
They follow leaders.
But haven't found their values.
They chase roles.
Without checking if it matches their soul.

Here's the truth:
Your greatest asset is not your degree, your resume, or

your LinkedIn profile.
It's your self-awareness.

Ask yourself:

- What kind of work makes me come alive?
- Do I enjoy leading or supporting?
- Do I recharge around people or in silence?
- What drains me—and what drives me?
- What values do I never want to compromise on?

Your answers may surprise you. They may even scare you. But they'll guide you.

Yes, industries evolve. Trends shift. Technologies change. But the one constant is you.
And the better you know yourself, the better decisions you'll make—about jobs, roles, relationships, and risks.

So before you try to master the world outside, take time to understand the world within.

When you truly know yourself, you don't just find the right job—you find the right journey.

Rooting for your inner clarity,
Ashish

CHAPTER V

First Job is Not Final Job

Dear Friend,

I know how it feels.
Your first job feels like a make-or-break moment.
Like this one decision will define the rest of your life.

Let me ease your mind—**it won't.**

Your first job is important, yes.
But it's not your final destination.
It's your starting point.

Too many young professionals treat their first job like it's a lifelong contract—one wrong move and everything will fall apart. But that's not how careers work. That's not how life works.

Your career is not a straight highway. It's more like a winding trail with detours, stops, climbs, and discoveries.

Some people start strong.
Others start slow.
Some love their first job.
Others realize it's not for them.
Both are okay.

What matters is not where you start—but **how you grow.**

Your first job is a classroom:

- You'll learn about deadlines, discipline, and decision-making.
- You'll understand office dynamics and unspoken rules.
- You'll see what you like—and more importantly, what you don't.

And that's valuable. Because clarity often comes from experience, not theory.

So don't get too attached to the title on your ID card.
Don't let one role define your worth or limit your ambition.
You are allowed to pivot. To explore. To evolve.

Just promise yourself one thing—**whatever your first job is, give it your best.**
Be curious. Be consistent. Be humble.
Not because it's the perfect job, but because you are becoming the kind of professional who brings excellence wherever you go.

Remember, your career is a book with many chapters.
This is just the first one.
The plot gets better.

Keep turning the page,
Ashish

CHAPTER VI

Learn the Art of Communication Early

Dear Friend,

You may have the skills.
You may have the degree.
You may even have the passion.

But if you can't **communicate** well—your growth will be limited.

Let me say this clearly:
Communication is not a soft skill. It's a power skill.

No matter what field you're in—engineering, design, finance, education, tech, sales—your ability to express your ideas clearly, confidently, and calmly will set you apart.

You may be brilliant at what you do.
But people won't know it unless you can explain it.

Learn to:

- Speak with clarity in meetings.
- Write with purpose in emails.
- Listen deeply during conversations.
- Present ideas in a way that inspires action.
- Ask questions when you don't understand—without feeling small.

Good communication builds trust.
Great communication builds influence.
And silent talent often gets overlooked—not because it lacks value, but because it lacks **visibility.**

This doesn't mean you need to become loud or extroverted.
It means you need to be **intentional.**

Practice speaking.
Volunteer for presentations.
Observe how great communicators talk—notice their tone, pauses, and simplicity.

Also, remember this—**communication is not just about talking. It's about connecting.**
It's about making others feel heard, understood, and respected.

Learn this early, and you won't just grow faster in your career—you'll build better relationships, handle conflict gracefully, and lead more effectively.

Speak not to impress, but to impact.
Write not to fill space, but to bring clarity.
Listen not to respond, but to understand.

Your words are your tools.
Sharpen them.

With clarity and care,
Ashish

CHAPTER VII

Don't Compare Your Chapter 1 to Someone's Chapter 10

Dear Friend,

You open Instagram.
You scroll through LinkedIn.
You see a post:
"Promoted at 25. Team of 30. TEDx speaker. Book author. Investor."

And there you are—on your couch, staring at your screen, wondering,
"Am I already behind?"

Let me tell you something that took me years to learn:
You are not behind.
You are on your own timeline.

What you're seeing is someone's highlight reel.
What you're living is your full story.
You may be in **Chapter 1**—they may be in **Chapter 10**.
And comparing the two is not just unfair—it's unwise.

You don't know the full picture:

- Their sacrifices
- Their sleepless nights
- Their failures they never posted

- Their privileges or their pain

Success isn't a sprint. It's a personal marathon.
Some people peak early. Others bloom late.
Some build fast. Others build deep.

Just because someone else is ahead on their path doesn't mean you're failing on yours.

Here's what actually matters:

- Are you showing up with consistency?
- Are you learning something new each month?
- Are you becoming a little better, wiser, calmer?
- Are you living with integrity, even when no one's watching?

That's progress. That's growth. That's your story unfolding.

Focus on your journey.
Celebrate your pace.
Trust your timing.

And when you feel the urge to compare, remember—**you are building something that lasts, not something that just looks good online.**

So breathe. Smile. And keep going.
Your Chapter 10 is still being written.

With patience and perspective, Ashish

PART II: The Career Game

CHAPTER VIII

Your Boss is Not Your Enemy

Dear Friend,

Let's be honest—most of us have, at some point, believed this:

"My boss doesn't get me."
"Too demanding."
"Plays favorites."
"Never appreciates."
"Just here to make my life harder."

It's a common feeling.
But here's an uncommon truth:
Your boss is not your enemy.

Yes, there are bad bosses.
Yes, there are toxic ones.
But most bosses are not out to destroy you.
They're under pressure too—handling expectations from the top, managing teams, balancing chaos, and making tough decisions every day.

Here's what will help you grow faster in your career:
Learn to manage up.
Not manipulate. Not flatter. Just understand and align.

Ask yourself:

- What does my boss value most—speed, accuracy, innovation, loyalty?
- What problems can I solve before they reach them?
- How can I make their job easier, not harder?

This doesn't mean you should tolerate poor leadership.
It means you should become someone who understands leadership.

Because one day—you might be in their shoes.
And when that day comes, you'll realize:
Being a boss is not easy.
Leading people is a skill.
And earning respect without fear is an art.

Here's a mindset shift:
Stop seeing your boss as an obstacle.
Start seeing them as a learning opportunity.

- From a tough boss, learn resilience.
- From a kind boss, learn empathy.
- From an unfair boss, learn how not to lead.
- From a visionary boss, learn how to inspire.

You may not be able to choose your boss.
But you can choose your attitude.

And that alone can change your entire experience.

Lead yourself well first. The rest will follow.
With wisdom and maturity, Ashish

CHAPTER IX

Promotions Don't Define Your Worth

Dear Friend,

In today's world, promotions are treated like validation. Your growth, your talent, even your worth seems to hinge on that one word: **Promoted.**

Get it? You're celebrated.
Miss it? You start doubting everything—your work, your pace, your value.

Let me tell you something important:
Promotions are recognition, not identity.
They reflect someone else's decision.
Your worth? That's defined by how you show up—every single day.

Don't confuse your designation with your **dignity.**
You are more than your job title.

I've seen brilliant people miss promotions—not because they lacked talent, but because of timing, internal politics, or a misaligned system. And I've seen average performers rise fast because they played the game well. That's the reality of most organizations. And while it may feel unfair, it also teaches you a powerful lesson:

Let external rewards be a bonus—not your only motivation.

Instead of obsessing over "When will I get promoted?"

Ask yourself:

- "Am I getting better at what I do?"
- "Am I trusted with more responsibility?"
- "Am I growing as a person and as a professional?"
- "Would I promote myself based on how I've been working?"

If the answer is yes—keep going.
Your time will come.
And if it doesn't come where you are—it will somewhere else.

One promotion won't make you, and one delay won't break you.
True professionals are driven by **purpose,** not just positions.

So don't let a missed promotion shrink your confidence.
Let it sharpen your focus.

You are not stuck.
You are being shaped.

And when the right moment comes—**you won't just be ready, you'll be undeniable.**

With pride in your progress,
Ashish

CHAPTER X

Switch Smart, Not Just Fast

Dear Friend,

The moment things start getting uncomfortable at work, the thought creeps in:
"Should I quit?"
You see people switching companies, jumping salaries, collecting job titles—and you wonder, "Am I falling behind by staying?"

Switching jobs is not wrong.
But doing it in a hurry, without reflection, **can cost you more than it gives.**

Here's the truth:
Sometimes, the problem is the job.
Other times, the problem is the mindset we carry from job to job.

If you keep switching every time things get hard, you might end up carrying the same lessons you refused to learn—into every new workplace.

Before you hit that "Apply Now" button, ask yourself:

- Am I running towards something, or just running away?
- Have I outgrown the role, or am I just bored?
- Is the culture toxic, or am I struggling with feedback and growth?

- Will the next opportunity bring me closer to my long-term goals?

Because here's the thing:
A higher salary doesn't always mean higher satisfaction.
A bigger brand doesn't always mean better leadership.
A new team doesn't always mean fewer problems.

The smartest professionals don't just switch fast.
They switch strategically.
They know when to wait, when to stretch, and when to walk away.

If you do choose to move, do it with grace—not frustration. Leave on a good note. Carry forward what you learned. And enter the next chapter with clarity, not just excitement.

Because your career isn't a game of musical chairs.
It's a journey of building credibility, capability, and character.

Switch when it's right.
Not just when it's easy.

With discernment,
Ashish

CHAPTER XI

Office Politics – Play it Ethically

Dear Friend,

Let's talk about the one thing everyone sees, no one admits, and most people fear:
Office politics.

It's there—in the hallway conversations, the unspoken alliances, the power plays behind closed doors.
You can pretend it doesn't exist, but you'll feel it.
You can avoid it completely, but it may cost you visibility.

So here's the real question:
Can you navigate office politics and still stay ethical?
Yes. You absolutely can—and you should.

Politics isn't always negative. At its core, it's about **influence, alignment, and perception.**
The problem starts when it turns manipulative or toxic.

Here's how to play the game without losing your name:

1. **Be aware, not paranoid.**
   Know the dynamics. Observe the networks. Understand how decisions are made. Awareness is power.
2. **Build genuine relationships.**
   Don't just network upward. Connect across teams. Help without keeping score. People remember authenticity.

3. **Let your work speak—but don't stay silent.**
   Do great work, yes—but also learn to talk about it.
   Visibility isn't arrogance. It's advocacy.
4. **Never gossip down to rise up.**
   Talking behind backs might win you temporary
   favor—but it chips away at your integrity. Stay clean.
5. **Choose diplomacy over drama.**
   You don't have to agree with everyone. But you must
   learn to disagree respectfully.
6. Stand your ground, but don't burn bridges.
   Sometimes, you'll need to speak up. Do it with facts, not
   fury. Firm, but fair.

And most importantly—**be so good they can't ignore you,
and so grounded they can't shake you.**

Office politics is a part of the workplace.
But your values? They're a part of you.
Protect them. Live them. Lead with them.

Play the game—but never forget who you are.

With strength and sense,
Ashish

CHAPTER XII

Be a Specialist with a Growth Mindset

Dear Friend,

In the early days of your career, you're told to be "a jack of all trades."
Try everything. Say yes to everything. Wear multiple hats.

That's great for learning. But at some point, if you want to grow,
you'll need to shift from being a generalist to becoming a **specialist.**

Why?
Because specialists are trusted.
Specialists are remembered.
Specialists are sought after.

Whether it's data, design, strategy, communication, finance, product, or people—**choose your craft and go deep.** Become someone who knows their domain inside-out, someone people come to when they want clarity, direction, and results.

But—and this is critical—**don't let your specialization become your limitation.**
That's where the **growth mindset** comes in.

You must:

- Stay curious beyond your niche.
- Learn adjacent skills that make you versatile.
- Be open to feedback, even when you're experienced.
- Adapt as industries evolve, tools change, and roles shift.

Your mindset will determine your ceiling.
You can be a world-class expert and a humble learner at the same time.

Here's the formula I believe in:

- **Depth gives you value.**
- **Breadth gives you flexibility.**
- **Mindset gives you longevity.**

So yes—be known for something. Be the go-to person in your field.
But also be someone who can learn, unlearn, and relearn—without ego.

Specialize with intention.
Grow with humility.
Evolve with time.

That's how you stay relevant—and irreplaceable.

With sharp focus and an open mind,
Ashish

CHAPTER XIII

Work on Your Personal Brand Every Day

Dear Friend,

You may not realize it yet,
but you already have a personal brand.

It's not your Instagram handle or your LinkedIn headline.
It's what people say about you when you're not in the room.
It's how you show up—in meetings, in emails, in conversations, in crises.

In today's world, **your personal brand is your professional currency.**
It opens doors.
It builds trust.
It sets you apart when everyone else looks the same on paper.

So here's the golden rule:
Don't leave your personal brand to chance. Build it with intention.

That doesn't mean you have to become an influencer.
It means you have to become **consistent, visible, and valuable** in what you do.

Start small:

- Show up prepared. Every. Single. Time.
- Be the person who adds clarity—not just commentary.
- Share your insights on platforms like LinkedIn—even if just once a month.
- Speak with authenticity, not just authority.
- Stay kind, even when you're right.

Let your work reflect excellence.
Let your values shine through your voice.
Let your online presence reflect the same person you are offline.

And remember—your brand is not about selling yourself.
It's about showing who you are, what you stand for, and how you add value.

People do business with people they **know, like, and trust.**
Your personal brand helps them do all three.

So don't wait for a promotion, an award, or a spotlight.
Start building your brand in the shadows.
Quietly. Consistently. Confidently.

Because one day, your brand will speak before you do.

With intention and authenticity,
Ashish

CHAPTER XIV

Upskill or Become Obsolete

Dear Friend,

The world is changing—fast.
Industries are evolving. Roles are shifting. New tools are replacing old systems.
What was relevant five years ago might be redundant today.

In this world, there's a harsh but honest truth:
If you don't upskill, you risk becoming obsolete.

You may have experience.
You may have talent.
But if you stop learning, the world won't wait.

You don't need to know everything.
But you must keep **learning something.**

The best professionals I know make learning a habit, not an event.
They treat online courses like workouts.
They read, not just to relax, but to grow.
They don't wait for their company to train them—they take ownership of their own development.

Ask yourself:

- What skills will my industry need 5 years from now?
- What tools are becoming standard in my domain?

31

- What do I feel insecure about in my role right now?
- What excites me enough to dive deeper into?

And then act on it.

Take a course. Attend a workshop. Read a book. Ask questions. Shadow someone smarter. Apply something new.

Learning doesn't stop at graduation.
It's a lifelong passport to relevance.

You don't have to master everything overnight.
But you do need to evolve constantly—because the professional who learns faster, adapts better, and grows deeper will always stay ahead.

Don't let comfort become your cage.
Choose growth over stagnation.

The world will reward those who stay **curious, committed, and current.**

With relentless learning,
Ashish

PART III: Mastering Life Beyond Work

CHAPTER XV

Don't Let Work Steal Your Life

Dear Friend,

Work is important.
It gives us identity, income, and impact.

But somewhere along the way, work has become **everything.**

Late nights have become normal.
Replying to emails at dinner feels expected.
Weekends blur with weekdays.
And somewhere in that constant doing, **living** takes a back seat.

Let me remind you of something simple yet powerful:
You work for a living. You don't live for work.

Yes, work hard. Be committed. Build something you're proud of.
But don't let your job consume your joy.
Don't trade your health, peace, and relationships for one more deadline.

Because no matter how ambitious you are—

- Your body has limits.
- Your mind needs rest.
- Your family needs you to be present, not just available.

I've seen professionals who got every raise and recognition—
but lost their health, their marriage, and sometimes, even themselves in the process.

That's not success.
That's survival dressed as achievement.

Here's what balance looks like:

- Logging off when the day ends—not out of laziness, but self-respect.
- Saying no to meetings that could be emails.
- Taking vacations without guilt.
- Spending time with people who recharge your soul—not just your resume.
- Pursuing hobbies that have nothing to do with your job title.

Work will always demand more.
But **you get to decide how much of yourself you give away.**

So protect your peace. Guard your time. Value your energy.
    Because when you look back one day,
you won't remember every meeting you attended—
but you'll remember the moments you lived.

Don't just build a career.
Build a life you actually want to wake up to.

With balance and boundaries, Ashish

CHAPTER XVI

Learn to Say No Gracefully

Dear Friend,

There's a reason you feel stretched thin.
A reason you're working late, juggling too much, and slowly burning out.

It might be because you haven't learned to say this one word:
No.

We say yes to avoid conflict.
To appear helpful.
To be seen as a team player.
To please our boss, our peers, even people who barely know us.

But every unnecessary yes is a quiet **no to yourself**—to your time, your peace, your priorities.

Here's the truth:
Saying no doesn't make you rude.
It makes you responsible.

You don't have to say yes to every extra task.
Every after-hours call.
Every event you're invited to.
Every favor that disrupts your schedule or drains your energy.

Learning to say no—**gracefully and firmly**—is one of the most powerful skills you can develop.

Here's how:

- Say no clearly, without over-explaining.
- Offer an alternative if you can: "I can't take this up right now, but I can review it tomorrow."
- Be honest, not harsh: "I'd love to help, but I'm at capacity this week."
- Respect your time as much as you respect others'.

People may resist at first. But eventually, they'll respect your boundaries—because you respect yourself.

Remember:
You are not paid to be available 24/7.
You are not obligated to carry everyone's load.
And you do not need to earn rest—it is your right.

Every no you say to things that don't serve you is a yes to things that do.

So practice saying no—kindly, calmly, confidently.
Your career will thank you.
So will your health, your relationships, and your inner peace.

With courage and clarity,
Ashish

CHAPTER XVII

Money Matters – But So Does Peace

Dear Friend,

Let's be honest—**money matters.**
It gives you freedom, security, and choices.
It allows you to take care of your family, invest in your dreams, and live with dignity.

There's no shame in wanting to earn well.
In fact, you should aim to grow financially.
But here's the warning most people miss:

Don't lose your peace while chasing prosperity.

What's the point of a 7-figure salary if your health is falling apart?
What's the point of a big house if you rarely feel at home?
What's the point of being rich on paper but poor in joy, time, and rest?

Money is a tool—not a trophy.
It should enable your life, not enslave it.

So yes, work hard.
Negotiate your worth.
Invest wisely.
Build wealth.

But also:

- Know when to log off.
- Protect your weekends.
- Guard your sleep.
- Spend time with people you love.
- Invest in experiences, not just possessions.
- Take care of your mind before you take care of your bank account.

And here's the ultimate truth:
Peace is the real profit.

I've met professionals who earn less but smile more.
I've seen people turn down high-paying jobs to protect their mental health.
That's not weakness—that's wisdom.

So build wealth, yes.
But don't forget to build wellness along the way.

Because in the long run, your peace of mind will always be more valuable than your paycheck.

With balance and intention,
Ashish

CHAPTER XVIII

Relationships Need Time, Not Just Time Off

Dear Friend,

You keep telling yourself,
"I'll spend more time with them this weekend."
"I'll call when things settle at work."
"I'll plan something after this project ends."

And the weeks go by.
The people who matter most slowly move to the margins of your calendar—pushed aside by meetings, deadlines, and the illusion that **time off** will fix everything.

But here's the truth:
Relationships don't thrive on leftover time.
They thrive on intentional time.

You can't expect connection if you're only offering attention when you're exhausted.
You can't build depth if all your conversations are squeezed between notifications.

Just like your career, relationships need:

- **Consistency** – showing up regularly, not occasionally.
- **Presence** – being fully there, not half-scrolling and half-listening.

- **Effort** – small gestures that say, "You matter to me."
- **Patience** – because every relationship has seasons, and none are perfect.

You don't need grand gestures.
You need small moments—daily calls, shared meals, honest conversations, undistracted quality time.

Because success means very little if you have no one to share it with.

So reach out to your parents—not just on birthdays.
Call your sibling, your friend, your partner—without a reason.
Be home—not just physically, but emotionally.

Don't let work become an excuse for emotional absence.

In the end, people won't remember your job title.
They'll remember how you made them feel.
Be the reason someone feels seen, heard, and loved.

Because when life gets hard—and it will—it won't be your boss or your promotion that gets you through.
It'll be the people you've invested in along the way.

With love and presence,
Ashish

CHAPTER XIX

Build Your Tribe – Network for Real

Dear Friend,

You've probably heard this a thousand times:
"Your network is your net worth."

But let's be honest—networking often feels like small talk in noisy rooms, business cards exchanged without intention, or LinkedIn connections that never become conversations.

That's not a network.
That's noise.

What you really need is a **tribe**—a circle of people who get you, support you, challenge you, and open doors not because they have to, but because they believe in you.

So how do you build that?

Start by showing up as a real person, not just a resume.

- **Be genuinely curious.** Ask people about their journey, not just their job title.
- **Offer help before you ask for it.** Add value, even if it's just a kind word, a useful resource, or a thoughtful message.
- **Stay in touch.** Not just when you need something—but when you don't.

- **Support others' wins.** Celebrate their success like it's your own.
- **Be honest about your own story.** Vulnerability builds connection far faster than perfection.

Networking is not about collecting contacts.
It's about **building connections**—deep, mutual, and meaningful.

Find people who:

- Uplift you when you doubt yourself.
- Speak your name in rooms you're not in.
- Tell you the truth, not just what you want to hear.
- Remind you of your vision when you lose sight of it.

Your tribe may be small—but if it's real, it's powerful.

And one day, when you're thriving, you'll remember the people who answered your late-night calls, believed in your wild ideas, and stood by you when the world didn't.

So stop networking to impress.
Start building to invest.

Find your tribe. Be a part of theirs. Grow together.

With authenticity and alignment,
Ashish

CHAPTER XX

Travel, Reflect, and Reset Regularly

Dear Friend,

Life moves fast when you're always in "doing" mode.
Emails. Meetings. Goals. Metrics. Repeat.

You wake up, get to work, chase deadlines—and before you know it, months pass. Sometimes even years.
And in the middle of it all, you forget to ask the most important question:
"How am I really doing?"

That's why I believe every working professional needs three things, again and again:
Travel. Reflection. Reset.

Let's start with **travel.**
Not just vacations for Instagram. I'm talking about changing your scenery to change your perspective.
When you step away from your usual environment—new thoughts, ideas, and emotions begin to emerge. You disconnect to reconnect—with yourself.
Then comes **reflection.**

Ask yourself:

- Am I happy with how I'm spending my time?
- Is this job still aligned with who I want to become?

- What have I learned lately—about my work, my relationships, myself?
- What do I need to let go of, and what do I need to pursue?
- We rarely reflect because we're too busy reacting.

But reflection is how you make sure your ladder is leaning on the right wall.

Finally, comes the **reset.**
You don't need to wait for a burnout or breakdown to take a break.
Resetting means restoring your energy, realigning your goals, and sometimes even reinventing yourself.
It can be as simple as a weekend alone, a solo walk, journaling, or a long, honest conversation with someone who knows your heart.

Pause is not weakness. It's wisdom.
Every high-performer I know makes time to unplug, rethink, and realign.
Not once a year. But regularly.

So take that trip. Block that time. Sit in silence. Revisit your goals.
It's not a luxury. It's maintenance—for your mind, your spirit, your clarity.

Because when you return—refreshed and realigned—you'll work better, live fuller, and move forward with purpose.

Take time to reset.

The world can wait.
Your peace can't.

With calm and clarity,
Ashish

CHAPTER XXI

Burnout is Real – And Preventable

Dear Friend,

You're not just tired.
You're exhausted—but pretending you're fine.
You're working, but the joy is gone.
You're delivering, but dreading every morning.

That's not a phase.
That's not weakness.
That's burnout.

And the scariest part?
Burnout doesn't happen overnight.
It builds up slowly—hidden behind productivity, masked by performance, and fueled by the pressure to always "keep going."

Let's be clear:
Burnout is real. But it's also preventable.

It begins when:

- You say yes when you mean no.
- You keep giving without refueling.
- You work from guilt, not passion.
- You blur the line between who you are and what you do.

The warning signs are subtle:

- You feel numb to things you once enjoyed.
- You lose motivation, even for things you care about.
- You sleep but never feel rested.
- You disconnect—from others, and from yourself.

So what can you do?

1. **Acknowledge it.**
   Don't wait for a breakdown to take it seriously. Burnout is not a badge of honor. It's a red flag.
2. **Set boundaries.**
   Protect your time, your energy, and your emotional bandwidth. You can't pour from an empty cup.
3. **Take real breaks.**
   Not scrolling-your-phone breaks. Real ones. Go outside. Breathe. Rest. Disconnect.
4. **Speak up.**
   Talk to someone you trust—your manager, a friend, a therapist. Silence only makes it worse.
5. **Reconnect with purpose.**
   Burnout often happens when your "why" gets buried under your "what." Revisit your values. Realign your path.

Remember:
You are not a machine. You are not a robot.
You don't need to earn rest. You deserve it.

The world glorifies hustle.
But a sustainable career is built on **balance**, not burnout.

So pause. Heal. Reset.
Your well-being is not a side project—it's the foundation of everything.

With compassion and care,
Ashish

PART IV: The Inner Journey

CHAPTER XXII

Build Discipline, Not Just Motivation

Dear Friend,

Let's be honest—**motivation is overrated.**
It's exciting. It's loud. It gets you started.
But it doesn't last.

One bad day. One missed goal. One harsh feedback—and motivation fades.
And then what?

That's where **discipline** steps in. Quietly. Steadily. Powerfully.

Discipline doesn't depend on mood.
It shows up when you don't feel like it.
It keeps going when no one's watching.
It delivers—not just once, but every time.

You don't need to wake up every day feeling inspired.
You just need to wake up and **do what needs to be done.**

Here's the truth most people miss:

- Motivation is emotional.
- Discipline is intentional.
- Motivation is a spark.
- Discipline is the engine.

You may not always feel like:

- Working out.
- Reading that book.
- Replying to that tough email.
- Updating that presentation.
- Practicing that skill after work.

But do it anyway. Not because you're in the mood.
But because **you made a commitment to yourself.**

Build systems, not just feelings.
Set routines, not just reminders.
Track progress, not just inspiration.

And don't aim for perfection—aim for consistency.

Because greatness isn't built in big bursts of motivation.
It's built in **small, disciplined actions repeated over time.**

So the next time motivation disappears (and it will),
let discipline take the lead.

That's how you win—at work, in health, in life.

With consistency and quiet strength,
Ashish

CHAPTER XXIII

Don't Lose the Child Inside You

Dear Friend,

As we grow up, we're told to be serious.
To be professional. Responsible. Practical.
And in the process, **we slowly bury the child inside us.**

The one who used to laugh without reason.
Ask questions without fear.
Dream without limits.
Feel deeply. Play freely. Express openly.

Somewhere between promotions and paychecks,
that child often gets lost—beneath calendars, deadlines, and
adult expectations.

But here's what I've learned:
That child is not your weakness. That child is your power.

When you lose that child, you lose:

- Curiosity
- Creativity
- Courage
- Lightness
- Wonder
- Joy

The most innovative people I know still play.
The most empathetic leaders still feel.
The most inspiring professionals still dream like children—with fire, with freedom, with belief.

So yes, be professional. Be focused. Be driven.
But also—

- Dance when no one's watching.
- Take joy in small, silly things.
- Ask "Why?" even if it sounds naive.
- Build sandcastles with your kids.
- Paint. Sing. Write. Wonder.

You are not a robot. You are a whole human being.
And the child within you is a source of aliveness that no title can replace.

Don't suppress it.
Protect it. Nurture it. Visit it often.

Because that child holds the version of you that wasn't afraid to be fully alive.

And that is the version this world needs.

With childlike joy and endless curiosity,
Ashish

CHAPTER XXIV

Your Definition of Success Will Evolve

Dear Friend,

When you started out, success probably looked like this:
A good job. A great salary. A fancy title. Maybe a corner office.

And there's nothing wrong with that.

But here's something you'll learn along the way:
Success isn't a fixed destination. It's a moving target. A personal journey. A shifting definition.

What once felt like "making it" might feel empty later.
What once felt small might feel deeply meaningful today.

At 25, success might be your first big promotion.
At 30, it might be work-life balance.
At 35, it might be being present for your child's school play.
At 40, it might be building something of your own.
At 50, it might be peace of mind.

And all of it is valid.

Don't let society trap you in a checklist.
Don't let LinkedIn fool you into chasing someone else's version of achievement.
And don't feel guilty when your desires and priorities change over time.

That's not confusion. That's **growth.**

So pause and ask yourself:

- What does success look like to me right now?
- Am I chasing this because I want it—or because I'm supposed to want it?
- What would make me feel proud and peaceful at the end of this year?

Define success on your own terms.
Redefine it when needed.
And give yourself permission to evolve.

Because the most successful people I've met aren't always the ones with the biggest job titles.
They're the ones who built a life that feels right—not just looks right.

So grow, shift, change.
Let your success story be yours, and yours alone.

With freedom and fulfillment,
Ashish

CHAPTER XXV

Find a Mentor, Then Be One

Dear Friend,

No one makes it alone.
Behind every successful person, there's often someone who guided them, challenged them, believed in them—before they believed in themselves.

That person is called a **mentor.**

In a world full of information, mentors offer something rarer: wisdom.
They don't just teach you what to do—they help you understand why it matters.
They save you from avoidable mistakes, expand your thinking, and accelerate your growth—not through shortcuts, but through insight.

So here's my advice:
Find a mentor. And then, become one.

Start with finding one:

- Look for people who've walked the path you admire.
- Don't chase fame—chase alignment.
- Ask for time humbly. Ask questions sincerely.
- Be coachable. Listen more than you speak.
- And when they pour into you, honor it with action.

But don't stop there.

Be a mentor too.
There's always someone one step behind you—confused, struggling, just like you once were.

Mentorship isn't about having all the answers.
It's about sharing your lessons, your scars, your stories.

You don't have to be perfect to help someone else grow.
You just have to care.

And something magical happens when you start mentoring others—
You grow even more. You reflect deeper. You lead better.

So always be in both roles:
The student and the teacher.
The learner and the giver.

That's how careers transform into callings.
That's how professionals become leaders.
That's how the ladder becomes a bridge.

Find a mentor who lifts you.
Be a mentor who lifts others.

That's the real legacy.

With gratitude and growth,
Ashish

CHAPTER XXVI

Keep Your Ethics, Even If the World Doesn't

Dear Friend,

You will be tested.
Not just on your skills—but on your **values.**
Not just by deadlines—but by decisions that ask:

"Do I take the easy way—or the right way?"

In the rush to achieve, impress, and climb, you'll see shortcuts.
People who bend the rules and still get rewarded.
People who manipulate and still move up.
People who compromise and still get claps.

You'll be tempted to do the same.
And that's exactly when you need to remember:
Your ethics are not situational—they're foundational.

Your reputation is not built on one big success.
It's built on **a thousand quiet choices**—when no one's watching, and applause isn't promised.

Ethics may not get you ahead overnight.
But they'll make sure that when you do get ahead,
you can look in the mirror and be proud of the person staring back.

Here's what I've learned:

Integrity makes you trustworthy—and trust builds long-term influence.

Doing the right thing may cost you opportunities—but it protects your peace.

Ethical people may move slower—but they move steadier, and they sleep better.

Don't sell your soul for a salary.
Don't trade your values for validation.
Don't confuse smart with shady.

Yes, the world can be unfair.
Yes, good people can finish last—for a while.
But in the long run, **character compounds.**
People remember those who stood firm when others folded.

So hold your ground.
Let your work be excellent, and your ethics unshakable.

Because success without integrity is empty.
But success with integrity? That's real power.

With strength and self-respect, Ashish

CHAPTER XXVII

Failures Are Detours, Not Dead Ends

Dear Friend,

You failed.

Maybe you missed a deadline.
Lost a client.
Didn't get that promotion.
Made a big mistake.
Or maybe, life just didn't go according to the plan you had
so carefully made.

And now, you're questioning everything.

Let me say this clearly—**failure is not the end. It's a bend.
A detour, not a dead end.**

Every successful person you admire has failed—publicly,
painfully, repeatedly.
The difference? They didn't let failure become their final
chapter.
They kept turning the page.

Here's what failure actually does:

- It reveals your gaps—so you can grow.
- It humbles your ego—so you stay grounded.
- It sharpens your focus—so you don't repeat the same
  mistake.

- It builds your character—more than success ever will.

Failure isn't the opposite of success.
It's part of the process.

So don't let it:

- Define you
- Deflate you
- Or stop you

Instead, let it **teach you.**

Ask:

- What can I learn from this?
- What would I do differently next time?
- Who can I ask for help or guidance?

And most importantly—remind yourself that failing at something doesn't mean you are a failure.

You're human. You're growing. You're figuring things out. And that alone is progress.

Keep going.
Keep showing up.
Keep believing that something better is ahead—not despite your failures, but because of what they taught you.

You've got this.
This is not your end.
It's a turning point.

With resilience and hope,
Ashish

PART V: Creating a Legacy

CHAPTER XXVIII

Work to Leave a Mark, Not Just a Resume

Dear Friend,

It's easy to chase titles.
To build a LinkedIn profile full of achievements.
To keep collecting bullet points for your resume.

But at some point, you'll realize—**you're not here just to fill a resume.**
You're here to leave a mark.

The world doesn't need more impressive profiles.
It needs more **meaningful contributions.**

Yes, your career matters. So does your growth.
But beyond the designations and design decks, ask yourself:

- What will people remember about working with me?
- Did I make my workplace better, or just busier?
- Did I help someone rise, or only climb for myself?
- Did I stand for something, or just survive silently?

Your legacy is built in the small things:

- The intern you mentored.
- The teammate you encouraged.

- The integrity you held onto during tough times.
- The extra effort you made when it wasn't required.
- The kindness you showed when no one was watching.

These moments may not show up on your resume.
But they'll live in hearts, in stories, and in impact.

Work with excellence, yes.
But also work with empathy.
Strive for results, but also for relationships.
Be respected not just for what you do—but for who you are.

One day, when the job titles fade and the applause quiets, what will remain is the **mark you left on people, projects, and the world around you.**

So work hard. Grow well.
But don't forget to **build something that outlives your job description.**

Make it count.

With purpose and pride,
Ashish

CHAPTER XXIX

Give Back Before You "Make It"

Dear Friend,

We often tell ourselves:
"One day, when I've made it... I'll give back."
When I have more time.
When I earn more money.
When I reach a certain position.

But here's the truth—you don't need to "make it" to make a difference.
You already can.

Giving back isn't about writing big cheques or building foundations.
It's about showing up for others in small, consistent, human ways.

- Mentor someone who's just starting out.
- Volunteer a few hours for a cause that matters.
- Share knowledge that helped you.
- Recommend someone for an opportunity they deserve.
- Listen to someone who feels unheard.

Your time, your words, your experience—they're more powerful than you think.

When you give back early, two beautiful things happen:

1. **You grow in empathy.**
   You begin to see the world beyond your bubble.
2. **You live with greater meaning.**
   Success becomes not just about what you achieve, but who you uplift along the way.

The world doesn't need perfect people—it needs aware people.
People who look around, not just ahead.
People who plant seeds, even if they may never sit in the shade.

So don't wait for a title or a bank balance.
Start now.
Where you are.
With what you have.
   Because giving is not a chapter that begins after success.
It's the very thing that makes success worth it.

Live in a way that lifts others.

With humility and heart,
Ashish

CHAPTER XXX

Your Story Matters – Live it Well

Dear Friend,

In a world full of noise, comparison, and constant pressure—
it's easy to feel like your journey doesn't matter.
Like you're just another name on a spreadsheet.
Another face in a crowd.
Another Professional chasing the next thing.

But let me remind you of something simple, yet profound:
Your story matters.

Yes—your story.
With all its imperfect chapters.
The detours, the doubts, the silent victories.
The days you showed up tired. The goals you quietly crushed.
The battles no one saw—but you fought anyway.

It all matters.

You don't have to be a CEO, a founder, or a viral success to live a meaningful life.
Impact isn't measured only in titles or trophies.
It's felt in how you live, how you treat people, how you rise and how you help others rise with you.

So live with intention.

Choose growth over comfort.
Lead with kindness.
Speak your truth.
Take risks that scare you and build a life that feels aligned—not just impressive.

And remember this:
Your story is still being written.
You hold the pen.

Write it with courage.
Edit it with wisdom.
Share it with pride.
Live it so fully that one day, someone else will find hope in your journey.

Because the world doesn't need perfect stories.
It needs real ones.
Like yours.

Thank you for showing up.
Thank you for growing.
Now go—
Live your story well.

With deep belief in your journey,
Ashish

A Final Word From The Author

Dear Friend,

Thank you for walking this journey with me—one letter at a time.

I didn't write this book because I have all the answers.
I wrote it because, like you, I've stumbled, struggled, succeeded, and still continue to learn every single day.
These letters are not instructions.
They are invitations—to pause, to reflect, to realign.

Being a working professional is not easy. You're constantly balancing ambition and anxiety, career and relationships, growth and stillness.
You're expected to have it all figured out, when in reality, most of us are simply trying to do our best with what we have.

If this book made you feel seen, supported, or a little more hopeful—I consider it a success.

My only wish is this:
Don't live on autopilot.
Build a life that's yours.
Make choices that feel right in your heart—not just on your résumé.
And never forget that you're allowed to change, evolve, and write a new chapter whenever you need to.

Because life isn't a race.

It's a story.
And you are the author.

Thank you for letting me be a small part of yours.

Stay honest. Stay hungry. Stay human.

With respect and gratitude,
Ashish

Write A Letter To Your Future Self

Dear Reader,

Before you close this book, I have one final request:
Write a letter to your future self.

Why?

Because life moves fast.
Because goals change.
Because it's easy to forget how far you've come, how hard you've tried, and how deeply you once cared.
Because someday, you'll need a reminder—from you.

This letter isn't for anyone else.
It's for the person you're becoming.
The one who'll one day be navigating new challenges, chasing bigger dreams, and looking back at today with fresh perspective.

Here's a simple way to begin:

Dear Future Me,

Right now, I'm at a stage where I'm... (write where you are emotionally, professionally, personally)

These are the things I'm proud of...
These are the things I'm still figuring out...
Here's what I hope you never forget...
Here's what I hope you've forgiven yourself for...

Here's what I hope you've grown into...
Here's the life I hope you're building—not just for success,
but for meaning.

And no matter where you are when you read this—I hope
you're still kind, still learning, still dreaming, still showing
up.

With belief,
Your younger self

You don't have to get it perfect.
You just have to be honest.
Seal it. Save it. Come back to it a year from now—or five.

Let this letter be your reminder that every version of you
matters.
That growth is not just about achievements—it's also about
awareness.
That the person you are today is laying the foundation for
the person you'll become.

Write it.
For closure.
For clarity.
For courage.

Because your future self will thank you for remembering
them today.

With reflection and hope,
Ashish

Journaling

Reflect. Realign. Reimagine.

Sometimes, the answers you're searching for aren't in a book, a podcast, or a meeting room.
They're already within you—waiting to be discovered through honest reflection.

Use these journaling questions as tools to pause, process, and gain perspective on your personal and professional life. There are no right or wrong answers. Just your truth.

On Career Clarity

1. What parts of my job energize me the most?
2. What tasks or roles feel misaligned with who I am?
3. If I could design my dream role today, what would it look like?
4. Am I building a career I chose—or one I fell into?

On Work-Life Balance

1. When was the last time I felt fully rested?
2. How often do I feel truly present with family or friends?
3. What boundaries do I need to set (or strengthen) to protect my peace?

On Growth & Learning

1. What skill am I currently working on (or avoiding)?
2. What was the last thing I learned that genuinely excited me?
3. What feedback have I received recently—and how did I respond to it?

On Purpose & Fulfillment

1. Why do I do the work I do—beyond the paycheck?
2. Whose life or work have I positively impacted in the past year?
3. What legacy would I like to leave behind at my workplace?

On Emotions & Mental Health

1. How often do I feel anxious, stressed, or overwhelmed?
2. What situations trigger self-doubt in me—and how do I usually cope?
3. When do I feel most confident and in control?

On Future Intentions

1. What do I want my life to look like in the next 3–5 years?
2. What's one bold move I've been delaying—and why?
3. What habits do I need to let go of?
4. What's the one thing I must start doing this month to grow?

How to Use These:

- Pick one each morning or week and reflect in a journal.
- Set a timer for 10–15 minutes and write without editing yourself.
- Revisit your answers over time—you'll be amazed at your own evolution.

Remember, growth begins with self-awareness.
And self-awareness begins with reflection.

You are your most important project.
Keep building.

With intention and insight,
Ashish